Second Edition

All the Tea in Chicago

BY SUSAN BLUMBERG-KASON

All the Tea in Chicago
Second Edition

ISBN 978-1-4243-3050-8

Designed by Joy Olivia Miller

Printed in Ann Arbor, Michigan
by Malloy Incorporated

Published in the United States by Des Voeux Press

Des Voeux Press
1529 South State Street
Suite 8B
Chicago, Illinois 60605
www.desvoeuxpress.com

Contents

Introduction

I guess I knew a good thing when I saw it. When I wrote the first edition to *All the Tea in Chicago* in 2006, I claimed in the introduction that Chicago was one of the best cities in the U.S. to drink loose leaf tea. Since then, tea has taken off in the Windy City even more than I could have predicted. The second edition of *All the Tea in Chicago* is written for the same reasons I decided to write the first edition: Chicago is a great tea city; tea is more popular in the city and across the country than ever before; and scientists are continuing to find health benefits to drinking tea.

Why a second edition to *All the Tea in Chicago*? The first edition sold out much quicker than I or the retail stores and restaurants expected. I needed to supply these vendors with more copies, but also had another issue to face—there were simply dozens of new tea houses and other sellers of tea in Chicago and its environs that weren't in existence when the first edition was printed. And, at the suggestion of fellow Chicago tea writer, Ceil Miller Bouchet, I am including commentary and recommendations for specific teas in the listings of this book.

The layout of this book is similar to that of the first edition. The first section is devoted to the hotels and restaurants that serve afternoon tea. I have renamed this section simply "Afternoon Tea" since more than just hotels serve it now. There are plenty of cafes and tea houses that offer scones and sandwiches which rival those at the best hotels on North Michigan Avenue.

The second section lists the tea houses and restaurants across Chicago and the surrounding suburbs that serve and sell loose leaf tea. For this edition, though, I have also included shops that sell high quality packaged loose leaf tea. For the tea houses and restaurants, again I have limited my listings to only those establishments that serve loose leaf tea. I have come across several cute and comfortable tea houses, mainly in the suburbs, that serve tea in tea bags. Because most restaurants do serve tea in this fashion, I have decided to omit those places. Loose leaf tea is a higher quality tea than that which is found in tea bags, which uses scraps and remnants of tea leaves. In the afternoon tea section, though, I have included Ethel's Chocolates even though they serve Tea Forte tea sachets, which uses a higher quality tea than what is used in most tea bags. I like their "tea for two" truffles and tea service, so have made an exception to the non-tea bag rule here. I've spoken to restaurant and café proprietors about the tea bag issue. It is my hope that they will switch to serving loose leaf tea in the future so everyone can enjoy a proper cup of tea!

Asian bubble tea has grown in popularity in Chicago even more since the printing of the first edition. I am including a revised and expanded section about Asian bubble tea in the third section. Some new cafes, as well as some older ones that weren't listed in the first edition, are found in this section.

The fourth section lists websites where you can buy loose leaf tea and tea accessories. With today's demanding schedules, many people prefer to shop online at their convenience, which is often during non-business hours. Many of these online tea shops have excellent toll-free customer service numbers.

Finally, I've kept the glossary and the indexes—both alphabetical and by area—in the fifth and sixth sections, respectively. As with any guidebook, the information is current as of writing so please call the tea houses or restaurants ahead if you need to know when they are open, if they still accommodate private parties, are wheelchair accessible, etc.

As always, enjoy this book and all the tea in Chicago!

SECTION ONE

Afternoon tea

Afternoon tea originated in Britain to hold people over between lunch and a very late supper, and is found in former British colonies across the world. In my early travels to Canada and New Zealand—British Commonwealth countries—I first tasted scones and tea sandwiches, washed down with cups upon cups of tea. Little did I know that afternoon tea was also served in my hometown of Chicago, mostly at the posh hotels along North Michigan Avenue. Twenty years later, more and more hotels in Chicago as well tea houses and restaurants have established afternoon tea as their own traditions.

Besides individual pots of loose leaf tea, afternoon tea service usually includes plated tiers of scones, finger sandwiches, and cakes and pastries. The scones are traditionally served with lemon curd, strawberry

ICONS

Use these icons to learn more about each entry at a glance:

child friendly

wheelchair accessible

available for private parties

near public transportation

wifi

preserves, and clotted cream, which is thick, whipped butter. The finger sandwiches usually include cucumber, egg salad, and thin slices of meat and salmon. Sometimes afternoon tea menus will not specify vegetarian alternatives, but most do have a nice selection of vegetarian sandwiches and other savories.
It's best to call ahead to confirm. Afternoon tea can be a satisfying alternative to lunch or dinner, and is a great way to enjoy the atmosphere of a five-star hotel without paying five-star prices. Afternoon tea prices average $25.00 per person at most downtown hotels and average $20 per person at free-standing restaurants and tea houses. It's best to call the hotels or restaurants in advance to check the price and hours of afternoon tea service, and because many afternoon tea venues require advanced reservations.

AMERICAN GIRL CAFÉ

This popular doll shop first opened in Chicago and is now known around the world. Afternoon tea is served in the Café for $17.00 per person, plus tax. The service begins with warm cinnamon buns and continues with delicacies such as blueberry-lemon scones, cranberry bread, lemon-poppy seed bread, vegetable cream cheese and cucumber sandwiches, chicken salad boats with cheddar cheese sails, egg salad sandwiches, and roasted turkey with cranberry mayonnaise. Tea service at American Girl Café concludes with fruit tartlets, cookies, and a chocolate mousse flowerpot.

At the time of writing, American Girl Place was in the process of renovating part of the former Lord & Taylor space at Water Tower Place (835 North Michigan Avenue, Chicago). They are scheduled to open their new doors in the autumn of 2008. Plans are underway to expand the Café to include a private dining area. The Chicago Avenue location will close after the Water Tower store opens.

In the city:

111 East Chicago Avenue, Chicago, Illinois
PHONE: 877.247.5223
HOURS: Afternoon tea is served daily at 4:00 p.m.
Reservations are strongly recommended.

??? DID **YOU** KNOW ???
About 80% of the tea served in the
United States today is iced tea.

CHALKBOARD

C halkboard started serving afternoon tea in December 2007 and is quickly becoming a city favorite! For $19.00 per person, it is good value for the money. Choose from more than a dozen varieties of Julius Meinl loose leaf tea to complement traditional tea sandwiches, scones, and pastries. Tea at Chalkboard is only served on Saturday.

In the city:

4343 North Lincoln Avenue, Chicago, Illinois
PHONE: 773.477.7144
HOURS: Saturday 2:00 to 4:30 p.m.

??? DID **YOU** KNOW ???
A single pound of tea will yield
about 180 cups of brewed tea!

CHESTER MANOR TEA ROOM

WEB: www.chestermanor.net

Wilmington is about an hour drive from Chicago and is located on the Kankakee River. With six types of afternoon tea service featuring more than a dozen types of loose leaf tea, the Chester Manor Tea Room is housed at the Chester Manor Bed & Breakfast, located in an Italianate style 19th century Victorian home. Their lightest tea service includes a pot of tea and a scone for $4.95 per person. Also on the light side, and for under $10.00 per person, is a tea service, which includes a pot of tea, scones, sweets, and—for a couple of dollars more—savories. The heavier afternoon tea services are named after British royalty and range from $17.00 to $35.00 per person.

In the suburbs:

116 South Kankakee Street, Wilmington, Illinois
PHONE: 815.476.1055
HOURS: Daily from noon to 3:00 p.m.
Reservations are required.

THE DRAKE HOTEL

WEB: www.thedrakehotel.com

When people think of afternoon tea in Chicago, many first think of the Drake. After all, the hotel is one of the oldest and most elegant hotels in Chicago. Located on North Michigan Avenue across from the Oak Street Beach, the Drake epitomizes the elegance of the Magnificent Mile. And its afternoon tea doesn't disappoint. It is served in the Palm Court on tables and couches surrounding a fountain, often accompanied by a classical harpist. Darker and more intimate than other hotels that serve afternoon tea, the Drake is particularly festive during the winter holidays.

Afternoon tea costs $37.50 per person, including tax and gratuity. The tea menu is extensive, including black, green, herbal, and fruit blends. A children's menu including a nice selection of decaffeinated teas is available.

The service is generally fine. They didn't accommodate vegetarians as well as some other hotels. Instead of appetizing meat-free alternatives, they simply provide extra cucumber sandwiches. The staff was good with wheelchair assistance, though. Private parties are not held in a separate room, but in the main area of the Palm Court.

In the city:

Palm Court
140 East Walton Place, Chicago, Illinois
PHONE: 312.787.2200
HOURS: Afternoon tea is served Monday through Friday from 1:30 to 5:00 p.m.; Saturday and Sunday 1:00 to 5:00 p.m.; Holiday season (Thanksgiving to New Years Day) 11:00 a.m. to 5:00 p.m.
Reservations are accepted for groups of eight or more.

ETHEL'S CHOCOLATES

WEB: www.ethelschocolates.com

Afternoon tea at Ethel's Chocolates is served all day and cuts right to the chase. Bypass the sandwiches and scones and dive right into the truffles for which Ethel's is so well known. For $15.00, enjoy "Truffles and Tea for Two", which includes tea and 10 truffles! Choose from a huge selection of truffles displayed in the front counter. Ethel's serves a variety of black, green, and herbal Tea Forte tea sachets.

In the city:

2 North Riverside Plaza, Chicago, Illinois
PHONE: 312.993.7515
HOURS: Monday through Friday 8:00 a.m. to 6:00 p.m.; Saturday and Sunday closed.

520 North Michigan Avenue, Chicago, Illinois
PHONE: 312.464.9330
HOURS: Monday through Saturday 10:00 a.m. to 8:00 p.m.; Sunday 11:00 a.m. to 6:00 p.m.

900 North Michigan Avenue, Chicago, Illinois
PHONE: 312.440.9747
HOURS: Monday through Saturday 10:00 a.m. to 7:00 p.m.; Sunday 10:00 a.m. to 6:00 p.m.

819 West Armitage Avenue, Chicago, Illinois
PHONE: 773.281.0029
HOURS: Sunday through Thursday 11:00 a.m. to 9:00 p.m.; Friday 11:00 a.m. to 11:00 p.m.; Saturday 10:00 a.m. to midnight.

3404 North Southport Avenue, Chicago, Illinois

PHONE: 773.525.1568

HOURS: Monday noon to 8:00 p.m.; Tuesday through Thursday 10:00 a.m. to 8:00 p.m.; Friday and Saturday 10:00 a.m. to 10:00 p.m.; Sunday 11:00 a.m. to 6:00 p.m.

In the suburbs:

20530 North Rand Road, Deer Park, Illinois

PHONE: 847.540.6107

HOURS: Monday through Saturday 10:00 a.m. to 9:00 p.m.; Sunday noon to 5:00 p.m.

527 Davis Street, Evanston, Illinois

PHONE: 847.424.0790

HOURS: Monday through Thursday 11:00 a.m. to 10:00 p.m.; Friday and Saturday 11:00 a.m. to 10:00 p.m.; Sunday noon to 7:00 p.m.

45 South Washington Street, Hinsdale, Illinois

PHONE: 630.794.0640

HOURS: Monday through Saturday 10:00 a.m. to 9:00 p.m.; Sunday 11:00 a.m. to 6:00 p.m.

28 West Jefferson Avenue, Naperville, Illinois

PHONE: 630.369.4189

HOURS: Monday through Thursday 10:00 a.m. to 10:00 p.m.; Friday and Saturday 10:00 a.m. to 11:00 p.m.; Sunday 11:00 a.m. to 9:00 p.m.

253 Old Orchard Shopping Center, Skokie, Illinois

PHONE: 847.675.7446

HOURS: Monday through Saturday 9:00 a.m. to 9:00 p.m.; Sunday 11:00 a.m. to 6:00 p.m.

FOUR SEASONS CHICAGO

WEB: www.fourseasons.com

The Four Seasons is a class act all over the world. And Chicago is no exception. Afternoon tea at the Four Seasons Chicago is one of the best I've tried anywhere and is served at small tables with oversized chairs and small couches, which makes the experience comfortable, relaxing, and elegant. The unique white tea pots are worth the price of afternoon tea, which is $25.00, excluding tax and gratuity. The Castle Cairn pots are made in Germany and can rest upright, at a 45 degree angle, or horizontally, depending on the where the tea is in its steeping process.

The Four Seasons serves a wide assortment of black, green, and herbal teas, along with a fine assortment of scones, finger sandwiches, French pastries, and tea bread. I was also very impressed with their vegetarian alternatives. The chef creates colorful and tasty savories that nicely complement the tea, scones, and pastries. To reserve a vegetarian meal for afternoon tea, call ahead.

Unlike other North Michigan Avenue afternoon tea spots, the Four Seasons has two private rooms, the Astor and Bellevue Rooms, to celebrate that special occasion. The Castle Cairn tea pots are not used in the private rooms.

In the city:

Seasons Lounge and Conservatory
120 East Delaware Place, 7th Floor, Chicago, Illinois
PHONE: 312.280.8800
HOURS: Afternoon tea is served Monday through Saturday. Seatings are from 3:00 to 3:45 p.m.
Reservations are required for the holiday season and are strongly recommended during other times of the year.

THE HERRINGTON INN & SPA

WEB: www.herringtoninn.com

The Herrington Inn is a lovely venue for a weekend away or simply an afternoon for tea. Tea is only served once a month and consists of traditional finger sandwiches, scones, pastries, and tea breads, all for $19.50 per person. For an additional charge, Atwater's serves champagne with their tea service. The setting is lovely and looks onto their garden area, which is beautiful year-round.

In the suburbs:

Atwater's
15 South River Lane, Geneva, Illinois
PHONE: 630.208.7433
HOURS: Afternoon tea is served on the third Thursday of every month at 3:00 p.m.
Reservations are required.

"As a rule they will refuse even to sample a foreign dish, they regard such things as garlic and olive oil with disgust, life is unlivable to them unless they have tea and puddings."
—GEORGE ORWELL

HOTEL BURNHAM

WEB: www.burnhamhotel.com, www.atwoodcafe.com

The Hotel Burnham is a quaint, boutique hotel located on State Street in the Loop, across from the old Marshall Field's flagship store (now Macy's). The hotel was designed by famed Chicago architect, Daniel Burnham. High ceilings, intimate banquettes, and potted palms define the elegance of the Atwood Café. The atmosphere is a peaceful oasis in the midst of the bustling Loop.

Contemporary versions of traditional tea sandwiches, such as goat cheese with sun-dried tomatoes, highlight the afternoon tea menu at the Atwood Café. A large variety of loose leaf tea is available for afternoon tea and other meals at the restaurant. Afternoon tea for adults is $20.00. For children, the cost is $15.00. The Atwood Café has a new private dining area that seats up to 40 people.

In the city:

Atwood Café
1 West Washington Street, Chicago, Illinois
PHONE: 312.368.1900
HOURS: Afternoon tea is served daily from 2:00 to 4:00 p.m. only from Thanksgiving to just after New Years Day.
Reservations are recommended for parties of six or more.

??? DID **YOU** KNOW ???
In ancient China, tea leaf pickers were not allowed to touch the leaves with their skin; they picked tea leaves with long finger nails.

INFINI-TEA

WEB: www.infini-tea.net

Afternoon tea at Infini-tea in Antioch—located near the Illinois/Wisconsin border—includes homemade scones with clotted cream or lemon curd, finger sandwiches, and mouth-watering desserts. They serve more than 60 types of tea blends, from black and green tea fusions to herbal blends to rooibos and oolong varieties. Antioch is probably the furthest tea shop from Chicago listed in this book. I'm not sure it's worth a special trip, but if you are in the area or have a craving for tea on your way to or from Wisconsin, Infini-tea is definitely worth the stop.

In the suburbs:

902 Main Street, Antioch, Illinois

PHONE: 847.395.3520
HOURS: Sunday through Wednesday 10:00 a.m. to 3:00 p.m.; Thursday and Friday 10:00 a.m. to 8:30 p.m.; Saturday 8:00 a.m. to 8:30 p.m.
Reservations are requested.

"I shall sit here, serving tea to friends..."
—T.S. ELIOT

THE INTERCONTINENTAL

WEB: www.chicago.intercontinental.com

The Intercontinental is a stately, old hotel on North Michigan Avenue, not too far from the Chicago River. Afternoon tea is served in the Zest Restaurant on Saturdays and Sundays during the year, and daily during the holiday season, and includes the traditional offerings of scones, finger sandwiches (including smoked salmon, tomato and cucumber, and turkey and cheese), and French pastries. The price for the regular tea service is $18.00 per person, which is quite a bargain for the location. For an additional $7.50, enjoy a glass of champagne with the full tea service.

The tea choices at the Intercontinental are not as extensive as those of other hotels along North Michigan Avenue, but still offer enough to suit most tastes. Choose from traditional English breakfast, Darjeeling, Earl Grey, Lapsang Souchang, black current, or orange pekoe. For decaf and low caffeinated teas, there is only a choice between chamomile and a naturally low caffeinated black tea.

In the city:

Zest Restaurant
505 North Michigan Avenue, Chicago, Illinois
PHONE: 312.944.4100
HOURS: Afternoon tea is served Saturday and Sunday from 2:00 to 5:00 p.m. During the holiday season, it is served daily, also from 2:00 to 5:00 p.m.

"You can never get a cup of tea large enough or a book long enough to suit me."
—C.S. LEWIS

THE JAMES HOTEL

WEB: www.jameshotel.com

Afternoon tea at the James Hotel is served in the sleek David Burke Primehouse. At $24.00 per person, the James Tea doesn't disappoint. The teas range from Chinese green dragonwell and blood orange to Japanese kukicha to Darjeeling, herbal and oolong varieties. The sweets and savories are advertised as "a modern alternative to the classic tradition" and include cucumber, apple, and radish canapés; truffle smoked tomatoes with goat cheese on a garlic crostini, mini dill and Himalayan salt popovers with salmon; financier "chips" served with pineapple mint salsa; preserved cherry clafoutis; chocolate canele; buttermilk scones with Earl Grey tea infused raisins; and carrot madeleines served with cream cheese fondue.

The crowd at the James is definitely young and hip, compared with that of other, more traditional afternoon venues around North Michigan Avenue. And if you really want to live it up, for an additional $6.00, enjoy a champagne upgrade with your afternoon tea service.

In the city:

David Burke Primehouse
616 North Rush Street, Chicago, Illinois
PHONE: 312.660.6000
HOURS: Afternoon tea is served daily from 2:00 to 5:00 p.m.

"Tea to the English is really a picnic indoors."
—ALICE WALKER

JULIUS MEINL

WEB: www.meinl.com/southport/home.html

Julius Meinl is one of my favorite tea houses in Chicago. Known mainly for its coffee and Austrian pastries, I quickly learned that it has an equally extensive tea menu. And, it now serves afternoon tea, which is a real bargain at $18.00 per person or $12.00 per child. The offerings for afternoon tea service include scones, tea bread, tea cookies, chicken salad on walnut bread, cucumber on white bread, smoked salmon on dark rye, ham on a pretzel roll, and a nice assortment of their delightful Viennese pastries. As for tea, you can choose from a large offering of black, black decaffeinated, oolong, green, fruit, rooibos, and white teas.

At the time of writing, Julius Meinl had not yet opened its Lincoln Square location, so please check their website for the hours and phone number of this new cafe.

In the city:

3601 North Southport Avenue, Chicago, Illinois
PHONE: 773.868.1858
HOURS: Monday through Thursday 6:00 a.m. to 10:00 p.m.; Friday 6:00 a.m. to midnight; Saturday 7:00 a.m. to midnight; Sunday 7:00 a.m. to 10:00 p.m. Afternoon tea is served Monday through Friday from 2:30 to 5:30 p.m.

4363 North Lincoln, Chicago, Illinois

THE LITTLE TRAVELER

WEB: www.littletraveler.com

The Little Traveler has seasonal afternoon teas, so please call for the schedule or check their website. These events feature speakers on tea, food, tea ware, and hospitality. The price of the tea service and lecture is $18.00, which includes a $5.00 voucher for purchases in the store that day. Located in an old Victorian house in historic Geneva, the Little Traveler is a maze of shops selling clothes, kitchenware, house ware, bath products, holiday decorations, jewelry, and antiques. Be sure the check out the tea room, which sells loose leaf tea, including the pretty, flowering Numi teas.

In the suburbs:

404 South Third Street, Geneva, Illinois

PHONE: 630.232.4200
HOURS: Monday through Friday 9:30 a.m. to 5:00 p.m.; Saturday 9:30 a.m. to 5:30 p.m.; Sunday closed.

??? DID **YOU** KNOW ???
You can brew more than 200 cups of tea
from one pound of loose tea leaves.

PARK HYATT CHICAGO

WEB: www.parkhyatt.com

Dining at the trendy, minimalist NoMi is usually no cheap affair. But, going for afternoon tea is actually a bargain here and still affords one the views of North Michigan Avenue and the luxurious atmosphere of the Park Hyatt and NoMi. The afternoon tea service costs $12 (not including the tea) and includes a three-tiered plate of finger sandwiches, petit fours, and pastries. The quantity and size of the food is smaller than that served at other afternoon tea venues in Chicago, but at that price, who can complain? The wait staff at NoMi is patient and courteous and willing to bring seconds of finger sandwiches to little people with large appetites.

As for the tea, NoMi's menu is extensive and ranges from a 1985 Royal Reserve pu-erh at $250.00 a pot to almost a dozen teas at $6.00 a pot, including Earl Grey, English breakfast, South of France rooibos, and sencha green tea, to name several. Other teas fall somewhere in that range, such as the 1949 Vintage Private Reserve pu-erh for $90.00 a pot and the Royal Himalayan Snowflake white tea at $30.00 a pot. The most decadent tea offering on the menu is a pairing of the 1985 Royal Reserve pu-erh with Frapin Cuvee Rebelais cognac. Pu-erh and cognac are quite nice together, but at $700.00, it's best to first know if you even like pu-erh! It's quite strong and has a smoky taste.

In the city:

NoMi Restaurant Lounge
800 North Michigan Avenue, Chicago, Illinois
PHONE: 312.335.1234
HOURS: Afternoon tea is served daily from 2:30 to 5:00 p.m.

THE PENINSULA HOTEL

WEB: www.peninsula.com

The Lobby Lounge at the Peninsula in Chicago was modeled after that of the original Peninsula Hotel in Hong Kong, complete with the little balcony off to the side of the Lobby that holds a string duo or trio. Okay, so Victoria Harbor doesn't loom across the street, but just off North Michigan Avenue, the Chicago Peninsula is every bit as elegant and luxurious as its older sister in Hong Kong. I love tea at the Peninsula because it brings me back to the place where I really learned to enjoy afternoon tea. The wait staff at the Peninsula Chicago is extremely polite, helpful, and very willing to bring seconds, thirds, and more of any of the sweets or savories served at afternoon tea.

Choose from one of a dozen or two black, green, herbal, or fruit blend teas and relax with finger sandwiches, scones, pastries, and a seasonal soufflé—all for $32.00 a person. A children's menu is also available, as are a la carte and champagne options. Private parties are very welcomed at the Lobby, but note that there is no private room, so you'll have to celebrate your special occasion in the midst of other diners.

On some Fridays during afternoon tea, the Peninsula offers informal fashion shows from Bloomingdale's, Escada, Giorgio Armani Cosmetics, Oilily, Pratesi, Ralph Lauren, and Yves Saint Laurent.

In the city:

The Lobby
108 East Superior, Chicago, Illinois
PHONE: 312.337.2888
HOURS: Afternoon tea is served Monday through Friday from 3:00 to 5:30 p.m.; Saturday 2:30 to 4:30 p.m.; Sunday 4:00 to 6:00 p.m.
Reservations are strongly recommended for the holiday season.

PICKWICK SOCIETY TEAROOM

WEB: www.pickwicktearoom.com

Frankfort is located south of Chicago and is quickly becoming a suburb of the Windy City. The Pickwick Society Tearoom serves a wide variety of green, white, black, herbal, and oolong Octavia loose leaf teas. Their afternoon tea service has three options: Marmee's High Tea for $25.00 per person, Afternoon Tea for $15.75 per person, or Breakfast Tea for $11.75 per person. Pickwick is also popular for children's parties and also offers three types of tea parties for the little ones. Check their website for special holiday afternoon tea services.

In the suburbs:

21 White Street, Frankfort, Illinois
PHONE: 815.806.8140
HOURS: Wednesday through Saturday 8:30 a.m. to 4:30 p.m.; Sunday noon to 4:30 p.m.; Monday and Tuesday closed.

"Tea, though ridiculed by those who are naturally coarse in their nervous sensibilities... will always be the favourite beverage of the intellectual."
—THOMAS DE QUINCEY

PINECONE COTTAGE TEA HOUSE

WEB: www.pineconecottageteahouse.com

The afternoon tea menu at Pinecone Cottage changes monthly. Serving a four course afternoon tea with a wide selection of loose leaf teas for about $19.50 per person, Pinecone Cottage also serves a Demi-Tea service for $16.00 per person. Check their website monthly for seasonal afternoon tea services, tea tastings, and cooking classes.

In the suburbs:

1029 Burlington Avenue, Downers Grove, Illinois
PHONE: 630.963.9130
HOURS: Wednesday through Friday noon to 4:00 p.m.; Saturday and Sunday 1:00 to 4:00 p.m.
Reservations are required.

"My tea is nearly ready and the sun has left the sky; it's time to take the window to see Leerie going by; for every night at tea-time and before you take your seat, with lantern and with ladder he comes posting up the street."
—ROBERT LOUIS STEVENSON

RITZ-CARLTON CHICAGO

WEB: www.fourseasons.com

Don't let the name fool you. Even after it was bought by the Four Seasons, the Ritz-Carlton Chicago is disappointing for afternoon tea. Held in the Greenhouse, the atmosphere could use some updating. I'm all for retro and old school décor, but the Greenhouse really left a lot to be desired. The tea service was acceptable, but not out of the ordinary, with finger sandwiches, freshly baked scones, pastries, and a wide assortment of green, black, and herbal teas. It does routinely receive high marks in newspaper and magazine reviews listing afternoon tea venues in Chicago. Standard afternoon tea service is $25.00. Add a glass of champagne or dessert wine and the price is $32.00 per person.

In the city:

The Greenhouse
160 East Pearson Street, 12th Floor, Chicago, Illinois
PHONE: 312.573.5154
HOURS: Afternoon tea is served daily from 2:30 to 5:00 p.m.
Reservations are strongly recommended, especially at the holiday season.

??? DID **YOU** KNOW ???
A cup of brewed tea typically contains less than half the caffeine of a cup of coffee.

RUSSIAN TEA TIME

WEB: www.russianteatime.com

At $22.99 per person for full afternoon tea service, you can't go wrong here. Crowded and sometimes noisy, Russian Tea Time has two rooms—one in the front with white tablecloths and comfortable banquettes and the other in the back with tables and chairs, adorned with Soviet propaganda art.

Afternoon tea is done Russian-style and includes savories such as cranberry and raisin scones with homemade whipping cream and marmalade; a salmon and cream cheese tea bite with fresh dill; crunchy spring crepes with peanut sauce; a roasted red pepper and cream cheese carré; a mini Rueben with farmer cheese and asparagus; a mini quiche with sun dried tomatoes; a petite napoleon torte; mini rugala; strawberry cake; and an assortment of traditional tea time cookies. The selection of teas is extensive and includes black, green, white, and oolong teas, as well as decaffeinated teas.

Private parties are welcome, but there is no private party room.

In the city:

77 East Adams Street, Chicago, Illinois
PHONE: 312.360.0000
HOURS: Afternoon tea is served daily from 2:30 to 4:30 p.m.
Reservations are strongly recommended for groups of four or more and on the weekends.

??? DID **YOU** KNOW ???
Tea brewed with loose tea generally tastes better than tea made from dunked tea bags.

SEASONS *of* LONG GROVE

WEB: www.seasonsoflonggrove.com

After the first edition of this book was published, I received many inquiries as to why Seasons was not included. How wrong I was to omit this afternoon tea venue! Seasons is located in quaint and cozy Long Grove, less than an hour from Chicago. Their afternoon tea service includes a choice of one of a dozen types of loose leaf tea, served along with homemade scones and biscuits, four types of tea sandwiches, and three kinds of finger pastries. Seasons is located in an old Victorian house and is a perfect site for bridal and baby showers. Check their website for their Mad Hatter Tea Party menu and price list.

In the suburbs:

314 Old McHenry Road, Long Grove, Illinois
PHONE: 847.634.9150
HOURS: Afternoon tea is served Thursday through Saturday from 2:00 to 3:30 p.m.
Reservations are required.

"When the tea is brought at five o'clock,
and all the neat curtains are drawn with care,
the little black cat with bright green eyes
is suddenly purring there."
—HAROLD MONRO

SERENITEA

WEB: www.sereniteanaperville.com

Call in advance for hours, as private events and holidays sometimes alter their business hours. Serenitea serves a wide range of loose leaf teas and also sells packaged loose leaf tea. They welcome bridal showers, baby showers, and other events. Prices range from $18.00 to $25.00 per person for private parties. Also check out their "Tea Parties to Go" catering option.

Their afternoon tea menu changes regularly, but includes a few types of finger sandwiches, a couple of types of tea breads, and several kinds of pastries.

In the suburbs:

3027 English Rows Avenue, Suite 107
Naperville, Illinois
PHONE: 866.327.3737
HOURS: Tuesday through Friday 10:00 a.m. to 5:00 p.m.; Saturday 11:00 a.m. to 4:30 p.m.; Sunday 11:00 a.m. to 3:00 p.m.; Monday closed.
Afternoon tea reservations are required.

??? DID **YOU** KNOW ???
Red tea or rooibos aids digestion and
is good for the skin. It is high in vitamins
and minerals and contains more
antioxidants than green tea.

SUZI'S TEA *and* CAFÉ

WEB: www.teavision.com

S uzi's Tea and Café recently relocated from Long Grove in the suburbs to Lakeview in Chicago. And what a great addition to the neighborhood it has been! Afternoon tea at Suzi's is served for parties of 15 people or more and reservations are required. For $28.95 plus tax and gratuity, the afternoon tea service includes an assortment of hot teas, fresh buttermilk scones served with Devonshire cream and strawberry jam, fresh fruit cups, assorted tea sandwiches, and an assortment of mini pastries. The tea also includes linens and flowers, so it's perfect for that special occasion, be it a shower or a birthday party. Afternoon teas are usually scheduled Monday through Friday at 4:00 p.m. For an additional charge, Suzi's will also provide host gift boxes.

In the city:

2965 North Lincoln Avenue, Chicago, Illinois
PHONE: 773.895.7408
HOURS: Tuesday through Friday 8:00 a.m. to 6:00 p.m.; Saturday and Sunday 8:00 a.m. to 5:00 p.m.; Monday closed.

??? DID **YOU** KNOW ???
Herbal tea is naturally caffeine free.

UNIQUE SO CHIQUE TEA & CHOCOLATE ROOM

WEB: www.uniquesochique.com

Walking into Unique So Chique, you'll probably just think you're in another cute clothing and gift boutique. But, once you enter the back room, you'll find yourself in a small, cozy tea room with several tables. The owners and wait staff are very knowledgeable about loose leaf tea and can make good recommendations for any tea drinker— pro or novice. The food served with afternoon tea is heavy on the sweets and lighter on the savories.

The shop in the front is also fun and a perfect place to buy a baby shower or host/ess gift.

In the city:

4600 North Magnolia Street, Chicago, Illinois
PHONE: 773.561.0324
HOURS: Afternoon tea is served Tuesday through Friday from 11:30 a.m. to 5:00 p.m.; Saturday and Sunday 10:00 a.m. to 5:00 p.m.

"I hire tea by the tea bag."
—MARTIN AMIS

VONG'S THAI KITCHEN

WEB: www.vongsthaikitchen.com

January is National Tea Month and Vong's Thai Kitchen kicks it up in Thai fashion. For $15 per person, the service includes pots of loose leaf Mighty Leaf Tea (displayed at the tables in test tubes to look at and smell before ordering) along with soup, satay, sandwiches, and sweets. Afternoon tea at Vong's Thai Kitchen is quite a bargain for the location and the amount of food, and is a nice change to the normal afternoon tea repertoire.

In the city:

6 West Hubbard Street, Chicago, Illinois
PHONE: 312.644.8664
HOURS: Afternoon tea is served only in January on Saturdays from noon to 4:30 p.m.

? ? ? DID **YOU** KNOW ? ? ?
By the middle of the 18th century tea had replaced ale and gin as the drink of the masses and had become Britain's most popular beverage. 96% of all cups of tea drunk daily in the UK are brewed from tea bags.

SECTION TWO

Tea houses, shops, and restaurants

Since the publication of the first edition of *All the Tea in Chicago*, at least a dozen new tea houses have sprung up across Chicago and the surrounding areas. This section lists those new establishments along with the others included in the first edition. I have also added more tea houses and restaurants that serve loose leaf tea in the suburbs. I kept suburban listings to those towns within an hour's drive of Chicago, although there are a couple of exceptions.

The tea houses in this section are casual, neighborhood places that offer more than the normal selection of tea bags at chain coffee houses. Some European cafes and tea houses chose Chicago as the first city in the US to set up shop. Others are based in Chicago and have expanded beyond the city's borders.

ICONS

Use these icons to learn more about each entry at a glance:

child friendly

wheelchair accessible

available for private parties

near public transportation

wifi

ARGO TEA CAFÉ

WEB: www.argotea.com

Argo Tea is quickly becoming the Starbucks of tea in the Chicago area. The philosophy behind this quickly growing tea house chain is that a new branch cannot open until the most recently opened branch is successful. So, although Argo's ascent into tea stardom in Chicago has been relatively quick, it has also been well planned and cautiously expanded. Argo is also treading new territory for tea houses in Chicago—going into the largest teaching hospitals in the city. With a kiosk in the University of Chicago Hospitals and in the new Northwestern Women's Hospital, Argo is bringing healthy beverage options to places that promote good health and should practice what they preach!

To see how Argo brews its liquid concentrations of tea that are served at its branches across the city and in the suburbs, visit the shop on Randolph Street in the theater district. Located in the former Noble Fool Theatre, this Argo café has upstairs seating and a nice panoramic view on the first floor of the huge tea vats that keep the tea at all the Argo branches flowing.

A somewhat recent convert to fruit blend teas, I especially like their hot or iced berry blast. Argo also serves signature drinks such as chai, Teappuccino®, Maté Laté ™, Tea Sangria™, MojiTea™, Hibiscus Steamer™, Pom Tea™, milky bubble tea with square-shaped pearls, and more.

Check Argo's website for more openings in the near future.

"The privileges of the side-table included the small prerogatives of sitting next to the toast, and taking two cups of tea to other people's one."
—CHARLES DICKENS

In the city:

---

958 West Armitage Avenue, Chicago, Illinois
PHONE: 773.388.1880
HOURS: Monday through Friday 6:00 a.m. to 11:00 p.m.;
Saturday and Sunday 7:00 a.m. to 10:00 p.m.

819 North Rush Street, Chicago, Illinois
PHONE: 312.951.5302
HOURS: Monday through Friday 6:00 a.m. to 11:00 p.m.;
Saturday 7:00 a.m. to 11:00 p.m.; Sunday 7:00 a.m. to
10:00 p.m.

140 South Dearborn Street, Chicago, Illinois
PHONE: 773.663.4471
HOURS: Monday through Friday 6:00 a.m. to 7:00 p.m.;
Saturday and Sunday closed.

16 West Randolph Street, Chicago, Illinois
PHONE: 312.553.1551
HOURS: Monday 7:00 a.m. to 9:00 p.m.; Tuesday
through Friday 7:00 a.m. to 11:00 p.m.; Saturday
8:00 a.m. to 11:00 p.m.; Sunday 8:00 a.m. to 9:00 p.m.

2485 North Clark Street, Chicago, Illinois
PHONE: 773.733.4231
HOURS: Monday through Friday 6:00 a.m. to 11:00 p.m.;
Saturday and Sunday 7:00 a.m. to 10:00 p.m.

3135 North Broadway Street, Chicago, Illinois
PHONE: 773.248.3061
HOURS: Monday through Friday 6:00 a.m. to 11:00 p.m.;
Saturday and Sunday 7:00 a.m. to 10:00 p.m.

5758 South Maryland Avenue, Chicago, Illinois
(inside the University of Chicago Hospitals, DCAM building)
PHONE: 773.409.4646
HOURS: Monday through Friday 6:00 a.m. to 6:00 p.m.;
Saturday and Sunday closed.

250 East Superior Street, Chicago, Illinois
(inside the new Northwestern Women's Hospital)
PHONE: 312.212.8144
HOURS: Monday through Friday 6:00 a.m. to 8:00 p.m.;
Saturday and Sunday 7:00 a.m. to 8:00 p.m.

1 North Dearborn, Chicago, Illinois
(in the Sears department store building)
PHONE: 312.212.8032
HOURS: Monday through Friday 6:00 a.m. to 8:00 p.m.;
Saturday and Sunday 9:00 a.m. to 7:00 p.m.

In the suburbs:

1596 Sherman Avenue, Evanston, Illinois
PHONE: 847.864.6909
HOURS: Monday through Friday 7:00 a.m. to 10:00 p.m.;
Saturday and Sunday 8:00 a.m. to 10:00 p.m.

??? DID **YOU** KNOW ???
Green tea helps protect against cancer,
lowers cholesterol, and aids digestion.
It is lower in caffeine than black tea.

ATOMIX CAFÉ

Atomix is a fun, retro café that is sure to suit tea enthusiasts of all ages. It serves about a dozen types of loose leaf tea, including genmaicha, Earl Grey, and English breakfast. You can order tea by the cup or by the pot. Enjoy baked goods from local bakeries along with sandwiches and healthy appetizers such as hummus and olive dips.

In the city:

1957 West Chicago Avenue, Chicago, Illinois
PHONE: 312.666.2649
HOURS: Monday through Friday 6:45 a.m. to 10:00 p.m.; Saturday and Sunday 9:00 a.m. to 10:00 p.m.

??? DID **YOU** KNOW ???
It's not unusual to hear someone in England ask for a "hot cup of cha" when ordering tea.

BEANS & LEAVES COFFEE & TEA

This café sells a wide variety of brewed loose leaf tea, along with packaged tea and tea accessories. If you go for afternoon tea at Seasons down the street, be sure to stop by Bean & Leaves for a pound or two of your favorite loose leaf tea. They also serve hot and cold chai, which goes perfectly with their chocolate chai caramels! If you are looking for fancy tea sugars, Beans & Leaves is the place to try!

In the suburbs:

320 Old McHenry Road, Long Grove, Illinois
PHONE: 847.821.0011
HOURS: Monday through Friday 7:30 a.m.
to 5:00 p.m.; Saturday 9:30 a.m. to 5:00 p.m.;
Sunday 10:30 a.m. to 5:00 p.m.

"Under certain circumstances there are few hours in life more agreeable than the hour dedicated to the ceremony known as afternoon tea."
—HENRY JAMES

BLUE PARROT CAFÉ *and* TEA ROOM

The Blue Parrot is a fun tea room and café that serves loose leaf green, organic English breakfast, and a peppermint organic blend tea. It has a children's area with games such as checkers and chess. The Blue Parrot also serves a healthy breakfast and lunch.

In the suburbs:

31 Forest Avenue, Riverside, Illinois
PHONE: 708.447.2233
HOURS: Monday through Saturday 7:00 a.m. to 3:00 p.m.; Sunday closed.

??? DID **YOU** KNOW ???
You should keep a tea bag in your first aid kit to soothe insect bites.

BOURGEOIS PIG

The Bourgeois Pig serves a large selection of loose leaf tea, which goes well with the healthy soups, sandwiches, and desserts on the menu. I like the Bourgeois Pig because it's located in an old house and has a cozy, warm feel. Frequented by DePaul students and Lincoln Parkers, it's often difficult to find a table on the weekend. Check upstairs for more seating. Although it's child friendly, there isn't much room for strollers inside.

The kitchen closes an hour before closing time.

In the city:

738 West Fullerton Parkway, Chicago, Illinois
PHONE: 773.883.5282
HOURS: Monday through Friday 6:00 a.m. to 11:00 p.m.; Saturday and Sunday 8:00 a.m. to 11:00 p.m.

"The morning cup of coffee has an exhiliration about it which the cheering influence of the afternoon or evening cup of tea cannot be expected to reproduce."
—OLIVER WENDELL HOLMES, SR.

CAFÉ AMBROSIA

Not to be confused with Ambrosia Café in Chicago, this Northwestern hangout serves more than 20 types of loose leaf tea as well as homemade Indian chai. The menu also features pastries, muffins, and cakes. During the cooler months, Ambrosia Café also serves soup and sandwiches. Live entertainment is performed when Northwestern is in session. An audio-visual meeting room is available in the café.

In the suburbs:

1620 Orrington Avenue, Evanston, Illinois
PHONE: 847.328.0081
HOURS: Monday through Friday 7:00 a.m. to midnight during the school year, 7:00 a.m. to 10:00 p.m. when school is not in session; Saturday and Sunday 8:00 a.m. to midnight during the school year, 8:00 a.m. to 10:00 p.m. when school is not in session.

??? DID **YOU** KNOW ???
Caffeine-free black teas are naturally decaffeinated by a high water pressure.

THE COFFEE *and* TEA EXCHANGE

WEB: www.coffeeandtea.com

This store is great for picking up that special gift, be it loose leaf tea or tea ware. Open for more than two decades, the Coffee and Tea Exchange is located in bustling Lakeview and sells more than 60 types of loose leaf tea. Although the shop doesn't have seating, they do serve brewed tea in paper cups to go. Check out the website for online shopping.

In the city:

3311 North Broadway, Chicago, Illinois
PHONE: 773.528.2241
HOURS: Monday through Thursday 8:00 a.m. to 8:00 p.m.; Friday 8:00 a.m. to 7:00 p.m.; Saturday 9:00 a.m. to 7:00 p.m.; Sunday 10:00 a.m. to 6:00 p.m. *The Coffee and Tea Exchange does not have seating.*

"If the artist must marry let him find someone more interested in art, or his art, or the artist part of him, than in him. After which let them take tea together three times a week."
—EZRA POUND

CREPE & COFFEE PALACE

This restaurant specializes in North African cuisine and serves a refreshing cup of mint tea. I love the warm and inviting interior, especially the Algerian art. Serving more than 30 types of crepes, Crepe & Coffee Palace is suitable for meals anytime of the day.

In the city:

2433 North Clark, Chicago, Illinois
PHONE: 773.404.1300
HOURS: Sunday through Friday 10:00 a.m. to 10:00 p.m.; Saturday 9:00 a.m. to 11:00 p.m.

? ? ? DID **YOU** KNOW ? ? ?
Elevation, climate, and soil are all growing conditions that will affect how a tea will taste.

DREAM *about* TEA

WEB: www.dreamabouttea.com

This Chinese tea house is warm and hospitable. Located in downtown Evanston, Dream about Tea serves a wide selection of Chinese green, white, red, black, and fruit blended teas. If you're looking for a Chinese tea set or tea ware, check out Dream About Tea or their online store. The shop also holds tea and Mandarin Chinese classes. Check the website for the current schedule.

In the suburbs:

1011 Davis Street, Evanston, Illinois
PHONE: 847.864.7464
HOURS: Tuesday through Saturday 10:30 a.m. to 8:00 p.m.; Sunday noon to 7:00 p.m.; Monday closed.

"If man has no tea in him, he is incapable
of understanding truth and beauty."
—JAPANESE PROVERB

F212

Named for the boiling point of water, F212 is a hip and fun dessert bar that serves over 25 types of loose leaf tea and tea beverages, including iced tea latte, black Indian tea with shaved coconut, and Chinese green tea, to name a few. For $12.00, enjoy "tea for two", which includes two refills of tea and two scones. F212 serves brunch on the weekends from 10:00 a.m. to 2:00 p.m. as well as lunch and dinner during the week. DJs spin at night and during brunch. F212 is also BYOB.

In the city:

401 North Wells, Chicago, Illinois
PHONE: 312.670.4212
HOURS: Monday through Friday 8:00 a.m. to midnight; Saturday 10:00 a.m. to midnight; Sunday 10:00 a.m. to 5:00 p.m.

??? DID **YOU** KNOW ???
You can use teabags as a compress
on swollen eyes.

FLAVORS *by* NORTH SHORE COOKERY

WEB: www.northshorecookery.com

Flavors, the gourmet store at North Shore Cookery, sells a wide selection of igourmet teas, including tea bricks—the traditional way of processing and serving tea back in heyday of the Silk Road. Flavors also sells tea ware, including tea pots, cups, and infusers.

In the suburbs:

600 Central Avenue, Suite 142, Highland Park, Illinois
PHONE: 847.432.1003
HOURS: Monday through Friday 10:00 a.m. to 8:00 p.m.; Saturday and Sunday 10:00 a.m. to 5:00 p.m.; open later for Ravinia concerts.

??? DID **YOU** KNOW ???
A single pound of tea will yield
about 180 cups of brewed tea!

*"Wouldn't it be dreadfull to live in a country
where they didn't have tea?"*
—NOEL COWARD

HI TEA

WEB: www.hiteachicago.com

Hi Tea is a wonderful addition to the growing eateries in the South Loop and serves more than 70 seasonal varieties of premium loose leaf tea from Japan, China, India, Sri Lanka, South Africa, Argentina, and the U.S.

Hi Tea sells and serves single region estate teas, black, green, white, and rooibos blends, as well as tasty tisanes, and floral and fruit blends. Try one of their tasty tisanes, which offers something for everyone with names like sweet almond cream and mint chocolate—definitely treats for people looking for something other than chamomile for non-caffeinated options.

Their menu features healthy soups, salads, hearty paninis, baguettes, and tea sandwiches. I particularly like the almond butter and jam sandwiches—a nice take on the traditional PB&J. The café is a good alternative to the noisy weekend South Loop brunch spots. The neighborhood has taken nicely to this new tea house, so there's usually a good mix of patrons ranging from college students, young professionals, and established residents in the community.

Hi Tea also sells vintage goods, gift baskets, tins of loose leaf tea, and tea accessories. You can order online for take-out orders, and the café offers a catering menu for larger needs. The space can be rented out on Sundays for private events. The hours can change on the weekends, so call ahead for the most up-to-date hours but whenever you get there—it's always time for tea.

In the city:

14 East 11th Street, Chicago, Illinois
PHONE: 312.880.0832
HOURS: Monday through Friday 7:00 a.m. to 9:00 p.m.; Saturday 8:00 a.m. to 8:00 p.m.; Sunday 9:00 a.m. to 7:00 p.m.

INFINI-TEA

WEB: www.infini-tea.net

This tea shop serves more than 60 types of tea blends, from black and green tea fusions to herbal blends to rooibos and oolong varieties. Infini-tea is located in quaint, downtown Antioch, about an hour north of Chicago, just south of the Illinois/Wisconsin border. Check their website for their online store and special tea events at their shop.

In the suburbs:

902 Main Street, Antioch, Illinois
PHONE: 847.395.3520
HOURS: Sunday through Wednesday 10:00 a.m. to 3:00 p.m.; Thursday and Friday 10:00 a.m. to 8:30 p.m.; Saturday 8:00 a.m. to 8:30 p.m.

"*Time for you and time for me, and time yet for a hundred indecisions, and for a hundred visions and revisions, before the taking of a toast and tea.*"
—T.S. ELIOT

JULIUS MEINL

WEB: www.meinl.com/southport/home.html

Julius Meinl is one of my favorite places for tea in Chicago (see also page 25 for information about afternoon tea at Julius Meinl). The friendly wait staff serves individual pots of tea along with a glass of water and either a piece of Julius Meinl chocolate or a tea biscuit on a little tray. I like to sit in the back area of the café, which has comfortable couches and chairs, along with booths and tables. The front area has a pastry counter, loose leaf tea and coffee beans for sale, along with other tea and coffee ware.

In the city:

3601 North Southport Avenue, Chicago, Illinois

PHONE: 773.868.1858

HOURS: Monday through Thursday 6:00 a.m. to 10:00 p.m.; Friday 6:00 a.m. to midnight; Saturday 7:00 a.m. to midnight; Sunday 7:00 a.m. to 10:00 p.m. Afternoon tea is served Monday through Friday from 2:30 to 5:30 p.m.

4363 North Lincoln, Chicago, Illinois

Meinl tea is also served at cafes across the Chicago Metropolitan area. These cafes include:

Jolane's
The new café at Abt Electronics in Glenview
1200 North Milwaukee Avenue, Glenview, Illinois
PHONE: 888.228.5800

Over Easy
4953 North Damen, Chicago
PHONE: 773.506.2605

Toast
746 West Webster, Chicago, Illinois
PHONE: 773.935.5600
and
2046 North Damen, Chicago
PHONE: 773.772.5600

Bamboo Blue
18147 Harwood Avenue, Homewood, Illinois
PHONE: 708.799.4700

Chalkboard
4343 North Lincoln Avenue, Chicago, Illinois
PHONE: 773.477.7144

The Gage
24 South Michigan Avenue, Chicago, Illinois
PHONE: 312.372.4243

La Sera
1143 North Wells, Chicago, Illinois
PHONE: 312.209.0791

KOPI—A TRAVELER'S CAFÉ

I love Kopi because it serves a great selection of more than two dozen types of loose leaf tea, but also brings me back to my days as a backpacker through Asia and Eastern Europe. Kopi is a traveler's one-stop shop, selling travel books, and artifacts, jewelry, and textiles from all over the world. It serves healthy choices for breakfast, lunch, dinner, and dessert—all of which are perfect with a cup of hot tea! The comfortable seating in the front of the café consists of cushions and low tables. Standard tables and chairs line the side and back of the café.

In the city:

5317 North Clark Street, Chicago, Illinois
PHONE: 773.989.5674
HOURS: Monday through Thursday 8:00 a.m. to 11:00 p.m.; Friday 9:00 a.m. to midnight; Sunday 10:00 a.m. to 11:00 p.m.

"There is a great deal of poetry and fine sentiment in a chest of tea."
—RALPH WALDO EMERSON

KOUKS VINTAGE CAFÉ

Kouks is a warm café located in the heart of Norwood Park. Surrounded by antiques and collectibles, diners can enjoy loose leaf tea along with pizza, pastries, and smoothies. The owners are friendly and knowledgeable about tea, so just ask them if you have any questions about their selection.

In the city:

5653 North Northwest Highway, Chicago, Illinois
PHONE: 773.594.8888
HOURS: Tuesday through Friday 10:00 a.m. to 6:30 p.m.; Saturday and Sunday 10:00 a.m. to 5:00 p.m.; Monday closed.

??? DID **YOU** KNOW ???
A serving of tea contains less than half that of coffee. Brewed coffee has an average of 110 mg. of caffeine per serving, while brewed tea has an average of 40 mg. of caffeine per serving.

LEONIDAS CAFÉ CHOCOLATERIE

WEB: www.leonidas.com

This chocolate conglomerate out of Belgium has a shop in Wilmette, one of its 1700 worldwide locations. The Wilmette store serves ten types of loose leaf tea and half a dozen blends. Come for the chocolate, stay for the tea!

In the suburbs:

1157 Wilmette Avenue, Wilmette, Illinois
PHONE: 847.256.5250
HOURS: Monday through Saturday 8:00 a.m. to 7:00 p.m.; Sunday 9:00 a.m. to 6:00 p.m.

"My experience... convinced me that tea was better than brandy, and during the last six months in Africa I took no brandy, even when sick taking tea instead."
—THEODORE ROOSEVELT

LOVELY BAKE SHOP

WEB: www.lovelybakeshop.com

Two words: mini pies. Well, maybe four: mini pies with tea. New to the Chicago scene in 2007, Lovely Bake Shop serves up delectable sweets that go perfectly with a nice, hot cup of tea. Enjoy a cupcake or one of their signature mini pies with a cup of Intelligentsia loose leaf tea. Lovely is located in an open loft space and is available for private parties, including tea parties! It also has a nice shop to buy that perfect host or hostess gift.

In the city:

1130 North Milwaukee Avenue, Chicago, Illinois
PHONE: 773.572.4766
HOURS: Monday through Friday 7:00 a.m. to 7:00 p.m.; Saturday 9:00 a.m. to 6:00 p.m.; Sunday 9:00 a.m. to 4:00 p.m.

??? DID **YOU** KNOW ???
Store your tea in a cool, dry, dark place, preferably in an opaque tin or jar. Store no longer than a year to prevent spoilage, deterioration, or loss of flavor.

MARRAKECH EXPRESSO

For Moroccan tea and tea smoothies, Marrakech Expresso is the place to go. Enjoy tea in a Moroccan setting on cushions on the floor in front, or on chairs and tables in the back and upstairs. Moroccan tea uses a lot of mint, so if you like mint, you'll love the tea served here.

In the city:

4747 North Damen Avenue, Chicago, Illinois
PHONE: 773.271.4541
HOURS: Monday 10:00 a.m. to 3:00 p.m. and 6:00 to 10:00 p.m.; Tuesday through Friday 10:00 a.m. to 10:00 p.m.; Saturday 10:00 a.m. to midnight; Sunday 11:00 a.m. to 10:00 p.m.

??? DID **YOU** KNOW ???
India is the world's largest tea producer.

METROPOLIS COFFEE COMPANY

WEB: www.metropoliscoffee.com

Edgewater is quickly becoming a hot neighborhood in Chicago and this café is one of its highlights. Don't let the name fool you. Besides serving a rich selection of coffee, Metropolis also brews up 35 varieties of loose leaf tea, including organic and fair trade selections. It also has soup, scones, muffins, and other pastries on its menu. Board games are available, as are comfortable and inviting upholstered chairs. Packaged loose leaf tea is also for sale here. For more information about Metropolis and fair trade tea, check out Metropolis's website.

In the city:

1039 West Granville Avenue, Chicago, Illinois
PHONE: 773.764.0400
HOURS: Monday through Friday 6:30 a.m. to 8:00 p.m.; Saturday 7:00 a.m. to 8:00 p.m.; Sunday 7:30 a.m. to 8:00 p.m.

? ? ? DID **YOU** KNOW ? ? ?
In ancient China, tea was originally prepared tea using bricks or cakes of dried, compressed tea leaves. They would make a powder from the bricks or cakes and use a whisk to blend the tea and the water. To this day, Japanese green tea is often prepared from a powder.

MOJOE'S CAFÉ LOUNGE

This Roscoe Village café has a fun, retro ambience and offers a wide selection of loose leaf tea. Mojoe's serves baked goods from area bakeries in a comfortable and inviting setting with mix-and-match sofas and chairs.

In the city:

2256 West Roscoe Street, Chicago, Illinois
PHONE: 773.388.1236
HOURS: Monday through Friday 5:00 a.m. to 7:00 p.m.; Saturday and Sunday 7:00 a.m. to 7:00 p.m.

"Take some more tea," the March Hare
said to Alice, very earnestly.
"I've had nothing yet," Alice replied
in an offended tone: "so I can't take more."
"You mean you can't take less," said the Hatter:
"It's very easy to take more than nothing."
—LEWIS CARROLL

MY PLACE *for* TEA

WEB: www.myplacefortea.com

My Place for Tea specializes in Chinese tea and sells loose leaf tea, bubble tea, and tea accessories. Come here to learn more about Chinese green, white, oolong, pu-erh, and black teas, along with other teas such as rooibos, yerba mate, Indian chai, and herbal tea. Check out their website for their extensive online store.

In the city:

3210 North Sheridan Avenue, Chicago, Illinois
PHONE: 773.525.8320
HOURS: Monday through Saturday 10:00 a.m. to 8:00 p.m.; Sunday 1:00 to 6:00 p.m.

? ? ? DID **YOU** KNOW ? ? ?
Tea may help strengthen bones.

NADA TEA *and* COFFEE HOUSE

WEB: www.nadateahouse.com

Nada is a relatively new tea house in Chicago, but it hasn't gone unnoticed. It was featured in the November 2007 issue of *Bon Appetit*, and for good reason. Nada serves a half dozen types of Japanese tea, including sencha, matcha, and genmaicha. It also serves chai, herbal teas, and a large variety of black teas. New on the tea menu is karigane, which is a green tea made from the twigs of the tea plant, not the actual leaves. The owner, Yumiko Kiyokawa, is very personable and enjoys talking to customers about Japanese tea. She recommends hojicha when eating sweets.

If decision-making is not your forte, try the tea sample set, which includes two or three types of tea. Sweets & Savories (see page 74) is down the street and works in collaboration with Nada for special events at the tea house.

In the city:

1552 West Fullerton Avenue, Chicago, Illinois
PHONE: 773.529.2239
HOURS: Monday through Friday 6:30 a.m. to 5:00 p.m.;
Saturday 8:30 a.m. to 5:00 p.m.; Sunday closed.

??? DID **YOU** KNOW ???
98% of people take their tea with milk,
but only 30% take sugar in tea.

PORTE ROUGE

WEB: www.porterouge.biz

Mariage Frerès is one of my favorite French tea companies and now there's a place in Chicago to find it! Porte Rouge sells everything French, including the above-mentioned loose leaf tea and tea accessories. From cast iron tea pots to individual tea infusers to porcelain tea pots with built-in infusers, Porte Rouge is a must for any Francophile and tea aficionado!

In the city:

1911 W. Division, Chicago, Illinois
PHONE: 773.269.2800
HOURS: Monday through Saturday 11:00 a.m. to 7:00 p.m.; Sunday 11:00 a.m. to 5:00 p.m.

"When one has tea and wine one will have many friends."
—CHINESE PROVERB

PROVENANCE FOOD *and* WINE

WEB: www.provenancefoodandwine.com

Provenance Food and Wine is a lovely gourmet wine and food shop, now located in both Logan Square and Lincoln Square. They sell Ineeka tea in pouches and loose leaf Serendipitea and Harney & Sons tea. They also sell blended teas from local Stellaria Natural Health (see page 102). Check Provenance's website for a listing of their many events and to sign up for their e-newsletter.

In the city:

2528 North California Avenue, Chicago, Illinois
PHONE: 773.384.0699
HOURS: Sunday and Monday noon to 7:00 p.m.; Tuesday through Thursday noon to 9:00 p.m.

2312 West Leland Avenue, Chicago, Illinois
PHONE: 773.784.2314
HOURS: Tuesday through Friday noon to 7:00 p.m.; Saturday 11:00 a.m. to 7:00 p.m.; Sunday noon to 6:00 p.m.; Monday closed.

??? DID **YOU** KNOW ???
Tea fights harmful bacteria and viruses.

SAVORIES

While Savories is a neighborhood coffee shop, it serves up a nice selection of loose leaf tea. Their soups and pastries perfectly complement one of more than 15 types of tea. Savories recently added some comfortable chairs and sofas. The shop also sells gift items, such as picture frames, coffee mugs, t-shirts, pot holders, and cards.

In the city:

1651 North Wells Street, Chicago, Illinois
PHONE: 312.951.7638
HOURS: Monday through Friday 7:00 a.m. to 4:00 p.m.; Saturday and Sunday 7:30 a.m. to 4:00 p.m.

??? DID **YOU** KNOW ???
Tea breaks are a tradition that have been with us for approximately 200 years.

SERENETEAZ

WEB: www.sereneteaz.com

The Western suburbs are definitely tea-friendly, thanks in part to SereneTeaz! This tea shop sells dozens of types of loose leaf tea, either packaged to take home or brewed to enjoy at the store or to go. Enjoy a pastry in the shop with that perfect hot cup of tea.

SereneTeaz is a one-stop shop for all your tea needs, such as gift packs of loose leaf tea, timers, tea kettles, tea sets, and infusers. If you can't get out to the Western suburbs, SereneTeaz also has an online store that sells all of the items listed above.

In the suburbs:

118A North Hale, Wheaton, Illinois
PHONE: 630.784.8327
HOURS: Monday through Wednesday 8:45 a.m. to 5:00 p.m.; Thursday 8:45 a.m. to 8:00 p.m.; Friday 8:45 a.m. to 5:00 p.m.; Saturday 9:00 a.m. to 5:00 p.m.; Sunday closed.

108 West Park Avenue, Elmhurst, Illinois
PHONE: 630.833.8329
Hours: Tuesday through Thursday 10:00 a.m. to 6:00 p.m.; Friday 10:00 a.m. to 8:00 p.m.; Saturday 10:00 a.m. to 5:00 p.m.; Sunday and Monday closed.

? ? ? DID **YOU** KNOW ? ? ?
Tea is a natural appetite suppressant.

SERENITEA

WEB: www.sereniteanaperville.com

Call in advance for hours, as private events and holidays sometimes alter their business hours. Serenitea has a wide range of loose leaf teas from India, China, Africa, and England. They also serve sandwiches and pastries à la carte. Check out their extensive online store at the website listed above. Serenitea also holds classes about tea at their café. For more information about their afternoon tea service, see page 34.

In the suburbs:

3027 English Rows Avenue, Suite 107
Naperville, Illinois
PHONE: 866.327.3737
HOURS: Tuesday through Friday 10:00 a.m. to 5:00 p.m.; Saturday 11:00 a.m. to 4:30 p.m.; Sunday 11:00 a.m. to 3:00 p.m.; Monday closed.
Afternoon tea reservations are required.

SHANGHAI TERRACE

WEB: www.peninsula.com

Shanghai Terrace is probably the nicest—and most expensive—Chinese restaurant in the Chicago area. It is decorated to resemble a 1930s Shanghai teahouse and doesn't disappoint in the tea selections—no matter your budget. Shanghai Terrace offers more than 30 types of loose leaf tea, ranging from $7.00 to $150.00 a pot. Dim sum, a Chinese brunch that consists of dumplings and other small plates, is offered every day, as are lunch and dinner, all of which are always served with pots of tea.

In the city:

Peninsula Hotel
108 East Superior, Chicago, Illinois
PHONE: 312.337.8888
HOURS: Monday through Saturday noon to 11:00 p.m.; Sunday closed.

"Thank God for tea! What would the world do without tea? How did it exist?"
—SYDNEY SMITH

SOUTHPORT GROCERY *and* CAFÉ

WEB: www.southportgrocery.com

I go to Southport Grocery for their out-of-this-world vanilla cupcakes and stay for the tea! The grocery part sells a nice selection of Harney & Sons and Rishi organic loose leaf tea. Choose from canisters of dragon pearl, white, green, red, or herbal teas. The Southport Grocery also carries SerendipiTea, which is not found in other stores in this area. So, whatever your taste in tea, Southport Grocery won't disappoint. And don't forget those cupcakes!

In the city:

3552 North Southport, Chicago, Illinois
PHONE: 773.665.0100
HOURS: Monday through Friday 8:00 a.m. to 7:00 p.m.; Saturday 8:00 a.m. to 5:00 p.m.; Sunday 8:00 a.m. to 3:00 p.m.

"There is no trouble so great or grave that cannot be much diminished by a nice cup of tea."
—BERNARD-PAUL HEROUX

SUZI'S TEA *and* CAFÉ

WEB: www.teavision.com

Relocated from Long Grove to Lake View in November 2007, Suzi's Tea and Café is a great addition to the neighborhood. Serving 135 types of tea, Suzi's is a cozy café that puts tea first and has a separate tea menu. Besides the black, green, white, rooibos, and herbal teas, Suzi's also has "no buzz" black teas in a dozen varieties. These teas are all caffeine free. The no buzz Darjeeling tastes just like its fully caffeinated counterpart. The white Darjeeling is also a house specialty. Tea, served in ceramic mugs with a strainer and lid, comes with a timer set for the time allocated for steeping your tea of choice. No time to dine in? Suzi's serves brewed tea to go and sells packaged loose leaf tea, tea pots, and tea ware.

Its food menu includes breakfast on the weekends and lunch during the week. The chai pancakes are popular, as is the oatmeal brulee—oatmeal with a caramelized layer of brown sugar and raisins served on the side. The lunch menu includes a soup of the day, fresh sandwiches, tasty salads, homemade scones with Devonshire cream, and other desserts. While Suzi's doesn't have a children's menu, many items are suitable for young diners. Suzi's also recommends two types of tea for children: root beer tea, made from rootbeer, wildberry, and herbs, and Greenzellah tea, which is made from green rooibos, strawberry, peach, orange, sunflower blossoms, and cornflowers.

Suzi's serves afternoon tea for parties of 15 or more and reservations are required. For more information about the café, check out their great website.

In the city:

2965 North Lincoln Avenue, Chicago, Illinois
PHONE: 773.895.7408
HOURS: Tuesday through Friday 8:00 a.m. to 6:00 p.m.; Saturday and Sunday 8:00 a.m. to 5:00 p.m.; Monday closed.

SWEETS & SAVORIES

Afternoon tea is served in this cozy and elegant Lincoln Park café by reservation only, usually around 3:00 p.m. Chef David Richards creates tea menus that include a variety of petit fours, tea sandwiches, and sweet breads.

Sweets & Savories sometimes teams up with Nada Tea and Coffee down the street for special events.

In the city:

1534 West Fullerton Avenue, Chicago, Illinois
PHONE: 773.281.6778
HOURS: Sunday and Monday 5:00 to 9:00 p.m.; Sunday brunch 10:00 a.m. to 2:00 p.m.; Wednesday and Thursday 5:00 to 10:00 p.m.; Friday and Saturday 11:00 a.m. to 2:00 p.m.; Tuesday closed.

? ? ? DID **YOU** KNOW ? ? ?
Apart from tourism, tea is the biggest industrial activity in India.

TAHOORA SWEETS & BAKERY

When my good friend, who hails from Pakistan, told me that she takes her friends and family to Tahoora for chai and dessert, I knew I had done something right by listing this Devon Avenue café in the first edition of *All the Tea in Chicago*. Tahoora serves a great cup of Indian chai, which is made from black tea, milk, half and half, and spices, and which makes an excellent pairing with a delicious Indian or Pakistani dessert, also sold in the cafe.

In the city:

2345 West Devon Avenue, Chicago, Illinois
PHONE: 773.743.7272
HOURS: Monday through Friday 10:00 a.m. to 10:00 p.m. (closed Friday 1:00 to 2:00 p.m.); Saturday and Sunday 9:00 a.m. to 10:00 p.m.

??? DID **YOU** KNOW ???
Tea helps regulate cholesterol.

TEA ESSENCE

WEB: www.teaessence.biz, www.teacraze.com

Tea Essence is a great addition to the Bucktown neighborhood. Serving more than 80 types of loose leaf tea, with a goal of stocking 150, Tea Essence specializes in chai and oolong tea. Their chai is made with almond, soy, or rice milk and is out of this world. Try their chocolate almond version of chai and you won't be disappointed. The milk oolong is unusual and quite delightful. They also serve tea lattes, using rooibos (red tea) and black tea. For Japanese green tea aficionados, the matcha smoothie is cool and refreshing.

The owners of Tea Essence plan to start tea tours, so check their website, www.teacraze.com, or phone them for more information about these exciting trips around the city, which will feature tea and dessert tastings, loose leaf tea shopping, and Japanese and Chinese tea ceremonies. They will also soon offer a Tea 101 class that meets for four weeks. Exciting developments for tea in Chicago!

In the city:

1913 North Milwaukee Avenue, Chicago, Illinois
PHONE: 773.276.2727
HOURS: Monday through Saturday 10:00 a.m. to 10:00 p.m.; Sunday noon to 8:00 p.m.

"It has been well said that tea is suggestive of a thousand wants, from which spring the decencies and luxuries of civilization."
—AGNES REPPLIER

TEA GSCHWENDNER

WEB: www.teagschwendner.com

Tea Gschwendner started in the late 1970s in Trier, Germany. It now has more than 130 shops across the world, in cities including Frankfurt, Vienna, Sao Paulo, Riyadh, and Chicago! Tea Gschwendner sells more than 300 types of loose leaf tea at each of its locations, including the two in the Chicago area. One of my favorites is the green passion fruit tea. It is light with just the perfect amount of fruitiness. I never liked fruity tea until I tried this tea and have not looked back.

Both locations sell packaged loose leaf tea, including black, green, oolong, white, rooibos, herbal, and fruit blends. The staff is all very knowledgeable and enthusiastic about tea. The shops also stock tea ware, including tea pots, tea warmers, filter systems, and customized tea gifts. The State Street location only serves brewed tea to go, but the Algonquin location has plenty of seating and serves sweets and savories.

In the city:

1160 North State Street, Chicago, Illinois
PHONE: 312.932.0639
HOURS: Monday through Sunday 10:00 a.m. to 7:00 p.m.

In the suburbs:

1624 South Randall Road, Algonquin, Illinois
PHONE: 847.458.8501
HOURS: Monday through Sat 11:00 a.m. to 9:00 p.m.; Sunday 11:00 a.m. to 6:00 p.m.

TEAVANA

WEB: www.teavana.com

Teavana is a national chain located only in shopping malls. It sells more than 100 types of loose leaf tea blends, along with tea pots, strainers, tea books, and other tea accessories. The staff at Teavana is very friendly and knowledgeable about tea. At any given time, Teavana offers about six types of tea for sampling. Although Teavana doesn't have seating in its shops, it does serve hot or iced tea to go. Check their website for more openings in the Chicago area.

In the city:

Water Tower Place, 835 North Michigan Avenue Third Floor, Chicago, Illinois
PHONE: 312.335.9802
HOURS: Monday through Saturday 10:00 a.m. to 10:00 p.m.; Sunday 10:00 a.m. to 6:00 p.m.

In the suburbs:

Northbrook Court, 2171 Northbrook Court Northbrook, Illinois
PHONE: 847.205.3333
HOURS: Monday through Saturday 10:00 a.m. to 9:00 p.m.; Sunday 11:00 a.m. to 6:00 p.m.

Old Orchard Shopping Center, 253 Old Orchard Center Skokie, Illinois
PHONE: 847.673.9611
HOURS: Monday through Saturday 10:00 a.m. to 9:00 p.m.; Sunday 11:00 a.m. to 6:00 p.m.

**Woodfield Mall, 5 Woodfield Mall
Schaumburg, Illinois**
PHONE: 847.619.4647
HOURS: Monday through Saturday 10:00 a.m.
to 9:00 p.m.; Sunday 11:00 a.m. to 6:00 p.m.

*"My grandmother died before tea bags.
I am grateful. My mother never admitted
their existence."*
—M.F.K. FISHER

*"We had a kettle; we let it leak: our not
repairing made it worse. We haven't had any tea
for a week... the bottom is out of the Universe."*
—RUDYARD KIPLING

TEN REN TEA & GINSENG COMPANY

WEB: www.tenren.com

When people ask me about Chinese teas in Chicago, I always refer them to Ten Ren. Although a national chain, it is probably the most well-known shop in Chinatown. Located in the older part of Chinatown, south of the Chinese gate, Ten Ren sells hundreds of types of Chinese black, green, and flower teas, as well as ginseng, tea cups, and tea pots. It also serves bubble tea. Seating is very limited.

In the city:

2247 South Wentworth Avenue, Chicago, Illinois
PHONE: 312.842.1171
HOURS: Monday through Sunday 9:30 a.m. to 7:00 p.m.

? ? ? DID **YOU** KNOW ? ? ?
True teas are made from the camellia sinensis plant. Herbal teas do not contain tea leaves, but are created from herbs and spices. Tisanes are made from fruits.

THIRD WORLD CAFÉ

Third World Café is the only cafe or restaurant in Hyde Park that I've found to serve loose leaf tea. It attracts students from the University of Chicago, as well as Hyde Parkers, both young and old. Third World Café serves organic tea, including Japanese green, black, peach jasmine, and herbal tea. Breakfast, lunch, dinner, and pastries are available seven days a week, and include a nice selection of vegetarian choices. Comfortable chairs along the windows and rotating local art are other attractions of this neighborhood café.

In the city:

1301 East 53rd Street, Chicago, Illinois
PHONE: 773.288.3882
HOURS: Monday through Thursday 7:00 a.m. to 8:30 p.m.; Friday 7:00 a.m. to 10:00 p.m.; Saturday 8:00 a.m. to 10:00 p.m.; Sunday 9:00 a.m. to 8:30 p.m.

??? DID YOU KNOW ???
Black and green teas are full of antioxidants, which fight cancer and heart disease.

TODD & HOLLAND TEA MERCHANTS

WEB: www.todd-holland.com

It's well worth a trip to this Western suburb for all its tea offerings. When some friends in the city told me they trek out here just for tea, I knew they were onto something good. Todd & Holland sells a huge variety of tea from all over the world: Indian black teas, Chinese black, green, white, and oolong teas, Japanese green teas, and all sorts of fruit and herbal blends. They also sell a superb selection of tea ware, including European and Asian tea pots and cups, tea books, strainers, infusers, and gourmet food. Their website sells all of the above and also lists events held at the shop. Todd & Holland is a must for any tea lover.

In the suburbs:

7311 West Madison Street, Forest Park, Illinois
PHONE: 800.747.8327
HOURS: Monday through Wednesday and Friday 10:00 a.m. to 6:00 p.m.; Thursday 10:00 a.m. to 8:00 p.m.; Saturday 10:00 a.m. to 5:00 p.m.; Sunday closed.

"Ecstasy is a glass full of tea and a piece of sugar in the mouth."
—ALEKSANDR PUSHKIN

TONI MARIE'S SWEETS & SAVORIES

Toni Marie's is known for its cakes, but it also sells a wide variety of packaged loose leaf tea in its gourmet section. According to Toni herself, tea has become an important part of the café. They use Treleela's spearmint lavender loose leaf tea in their iced tea. Look for listings of seasonal brewed teas on their chalkboard menu behind the counter. Not all the teas use loose leaf tea, so ask before you order. Located near the Metra station in Hinsdale, Toni Marie's is a great place to grab a cup of tea, a sandwich, or a delicious piece of cake. During the warm months, there is ample outdoor seating in front of the café.

In the suburbs:

51 South Washington Avenue, Hinsdale, Illinois
PHONE: 630.789.2020
WEB: www.tonisweets.com
HOURS: Monday through Friday 6:00 a.m. to 6:00 p.m.; Saturday 6:00 a.m. to 5:00 p.m.; Sunday 7:00 a.m. to 1:00 p.m.

??? DID **YOU** KNOW ???
Drinking green tea may help
maintain cartilage.

SECTION THREE

Bubble tea

Bubble tea took Taiwan and Hong Kong by storm in the 1990s and is now popular in the Chinatowns—and beyond—across the U.S., including Chicago's Chinatown on the south side and Argyle Street on the north side. Made from tea, milk, sugar, and giant black tapioca balls, bubble tea gets its name not from the tapioca balls, but from the foam that forms from shaking the freshly brewed tea with ice. Also known as pearl tea, this refreshing drink comes in different fruit flavors and colors and is served with a fat straw.

ICONS

Use these icons to learn more about each entry at a glance:

child friendly

wheelchair accessible

available for private parties

near public transportation

wifi

ARGO TEA CAFÉ

WEB: www.argotea.com

Bubble tea at Argo is unique. Instead of serving it with round tapioca pearls, Argo uses square shaped chewy pearls. Argo also serves signature cold tea drinks such as Tea Sangria™, MojiTea™, Hibiscus Steamer™, Pom Tea™, Smootea, and Teappuccino®. For more information on Argo, see page 40.

In the city:

958 West Armitage Avenue, Chicago, Illinois
PHONE: 773.388.1880
HOURS: Monday through Friday 6:00 a.m. to 11:00 p.m.;
Saturday and Sunday 7:00 a.m. to 10:00 p.m.

819 North Rush Street, Chicago, Illinois
PHONE: 312.951.5302
HOURS: Monday through Friday 6:00 a.m.
to 11:00 p.m.; Saturday 7:00 a.m. to 11:00 p.m.;
Sunday 7:00 a.m. to 10:00 p.m.

140 South Dearborn Street, Chicago, Illinois
PHONE: 773.663.4471
HOURS: Monday through Friday 6:00 a.m. to 7:00 p.m.;
Saturday and Sunday closed.

16 West Randolph Street, Chicago, Illinois
PHONE: 312.553.1551
HOURS: Monday 7:00 a.m. to 9:00 p.m.; Tuesday
through Friday 7:00 a.m. to 11:00 p.m.; Saturday
8:00 a.m. to 11:00 p.m.; Sunday 8:00 a.m. to 9:00 p.m.

2485 North Clark Street, Chicago, Illinois
PHONE: 773.733.4231
HOURS: Monday through Friday 6:00 a.m. to 11:00 p.m.;
Saturday and Sunday 7:00 a.m. to 10:00 p.m.

3135 North Broadway Street, Chicago, Illinois
PHONE: 773.248.3061
HOURS: Monday through Friday 6:00 a.m. to 11:00 p.m.;
Saturday and Sunday 7:00 a.m. to 10:00 p.m.

5758 South Maryland Avenue, Chicago, Illinois
(inside the University of Chicago Hospitals, DCAM building)
PHONE: 773.409.4646
HOURS: Monday through Friday 6:00 a.m. to 6:00 p.m.;
Saturday and Sunday closed.

250 East Superior Street, Chicago, Illinois
(inside the new Northwestern Women's Hospital)
PHONE: 312.212.8144
HOURS: Monday through Friday 6:00 a.m. to 8:00 p.m.;
Saturday and Sunday 7:00 a.m. to 8:00 p.m.

1 North Dearborn, Chicago, Illinois
(in the Sears department store building)
PHONE: 312.212.8032
HOURS: Monday through Friday 6:00 a.m. to 8:00 p.m.;
Saturday and Sunday 9:00 a.m. to 7:00 p.m.

In the suburbs:

1596 Sherman Ave, Evanston, Illinois
PHONE: 847.864.6909
HOURS: Monday through Friday 7:00 a.m. to 10:00 p.m.;
Saturday and Sunday 8:00 a.m. to 10:00 p.m.

BEBOBA BUBBLE TEA HOUSE

WEB: www.beboba.com

This bubble tea shop is brightly decorated and has a selection of board games to play while enjoying your drink. BeBoBa has more than 50 types of bubble tea without mixing ingredients, which can be combined to make an even wider selection.

In the city:

3533-B North Western Avenue, Chicago, Illinois
PHONE: 773.883.2622
HOURS: Monday through Thursday 10:00 a.m.
to 8:00 p.m.; Friday 10:00 a.m. to 9:00 p.m.;
Saturday noon to 9:00 p.m.; Sunday closed.

??? DID **YOU** KNOW ???
Oolong tea aids digestion and is good
for the skin and teeth.

BOBA BEE

Boba Bee serves more than 40 types of bubble tea, including avocado, lychee, passion fruit, papaya, and taro—a purplish root vegetable popular in Asia, especially in desserts. It also serves ice cream and milkshakes.

In the city:

5868 North Lincoln Avenue, Chicago, Illinois
PHONE: 773.572.7175
HOURS: Monday through Friday 9:00 a.m. to 10:00 p.m.; Saturday 10:00 a.m. to 10:00 p.m.; Sunday 10:00 a.m. to 7:00 p.m.

"The glacier knocks in the cupboard,
the desert sighs in the bed, and the crack in the
tea-cup opens a lane to the land of the dead."
—W.H. AUDEN

CHILL BUBBLE TEA

WEB: www.chillbubbletea.com

This rapidly expanding bubble tea shop carries more than 80 types of bubble tea, including popular flavors such as banana, strawberry, cherry, and chocolate. Check out their website for new locations, including those listed above in downtown Chicago, in the Gurnee Mills Mall, and on the campus of Northwestern University.

In the suburbs:

6317 West Dempster Street, Morton Grove, Illinois
PHONE: 847.967.0911
HOURS: Sunday through Thursday noon to 11:00 p.m.; Friday and Saturday noon to 1:00 a.m.

Stratford Square Shopping Mall
152 Stratford Square Mall #D4, Bloomingdale, Illinois
PHONE: 630.539.1306
HOURS: Monday through Saturday 10:00 a.m. to 9:00 p.m.; Sunday 11:00 a.m. to 6:00 p.m.

Woodfield Shopping Mall
F-319 Woodfield Mall, Schaumburg, Illinois
PHONE: 847.619.1305
HOURS: Monday through Saturday 10:00 a.m. to 9:00 p.m.; Sunday 11:00 a.m. to 6:00 p.m.

COMING SOON:
Locations in downtown Chicago, Gurnee Mills, and Northwestern University

HAI YEN

Hai Yen is one of my favorite Vietnamese restaurants located in "New Chinatown", an area on the north side of Chicago that was settled 20 to 30 years ago by ethnic Chinese from Vietnam, Cambodia, and Laos. And now Hai Yen has a second location in Lincoln Park, which also offers a wide selection of bubble tea.

In the city:

1055 West Argyle Street, Chicago, Illinois
PHONE: 773.561.4077
HOURS: Monday, Tuesday, and Thursday 10:30 a.m. to 10:00 p.m.; Friday and Saturday 10:30 a.m. to 10:30 p.m.; Sunday 9:30 a.m. to 10:00 p.m.; Wednesday closed.

2723 North Clark Street, Chicago, Illinois
PHONE: 773.868.4888
HOURS: Monday, Tuesday, and Thursday 10:30 a.m. to 10:00 p.m.; Friday 10:30 a.m. to 10:30 p.m.; Saturday 9:30 a.m. to 10:30 p.m.; Sunday 9:30 a.m. to 10:00 p.m.

??? DID YOU KNOW ???
Did you know that green tea contains many vitamins and minerals?

JAVA BUBBLES TEA HOUSE

Java Bubbles Tea House serves more than 50 types of drinks, including bubble tea, milk tea, and hot tea. Never tried jack fruit? Now's your chance. The variety of fruit flavors is extensive. Sweet and savory treats are also included on the menu.

In the city:

5108 North Broadway Street, Chicago, Illinois
PHONE: 773.944.0110
HOURS: Daily 8:00 a.m. to 8:00 p.m.

??? DID **YOU** KNOW ???
Infusing tea leaves in a tea pot became
a widespread practice in China early during
the Ming dynasty.

JOY YEE'S NOODLE SHOP

WEB: www.joyyee.com

Joy Yee is known for its wide selection of bubble tea as well as tasty Asian noodle dishes. The 2159 South China Place location has a window separate from the restaurant for ordering bubble tea to go. The expanded Chinatown location at 2139 South China Place also offers a party room and seasonal outdoor seating. Joy Yee is popular among younger crowds and families.

In the city:

2159 South China Place
Chinatown Square, Chicago, Illinois
PHONE: 312.328.0001
HOURS: Daily 11:00 a.m. to 10:30 p.m.

2139 South China Place
Chinatown Square, Chicago, Illinois
PHONE: 312.328.0001
HOURS: Daily 11:00 a.m. to 10:30 p.m.

1335 South Halsted, Chicago, Illinois
PHONE: 312.997.2128
HOURS: Monday through Thursday 11:30 a.m. to 10:30 p.m.; Friday and Saturday 11:30 a.m. to 11:00 p.m.; Sunday noon to 10:00 p.m.

In the suburbs:

---

521 Davis Street, Evanston, Illinois
PHONE: 847.733.1900
HOURS: Monday through Thursday 11:30 a.m.
to 10:00 p.m.; Friday and Saturday 11:30 a.m.
to 10:30 p.m.; Sunday noon to 10:00 p.m.

1163 E. Ogden Avenue, Naperville, Illinois
PHONE: 630.579.6800
HOURS: Monday through Thursday 11:30 a.m.
to 9:00 p.m.; Friday and Saturday 11:30 a.m.
to 10:00 p.m.; Sunday noon to 9:00 p.m.

SAINT ANNA BAKERY & CAFÉ

Saint Anna is a modest Hong Kong style bakery that serves more than 35 types of bubble tea. It also sells whipped cream and fruit filled Western style cakes, Chinese sticky rice desserts, and a wide assortment of filled buns that range from ham and egg to sweet red bean paste. Saint Anna gets crowded on the weekends, so be prepared to wait for a table Hong Kong style—hovering above diners while they finish eating so you can secure their table as soon as they stand up to leave.

In the city:

2158 South Archer, Chicago, Illinois
PHONE: 312.225.3168
HOURS: Daily 8:00 a.m. to 8:00 p.m.

??? DID **YOU** KNOW ???
Did you know that oolong and green teas
help boost the metabolism?

ST. ALP'S TEA HOUSE

WEB: www.saints-alp.com.hk

St. Alp's started in Hong Kong while I lived there in the 1990s, but really expanded after I left—including opening a location in Chicago's Chinatown! Serving more than 70 types of tea drinks, including bubble tea, mung bean tea drinks, and milk tea drinks, St. Alp's also has an extensive "snack" menu, with offerings like dumplings, teriyaki chicken, and rice and noodle dishes—enough options to make full meals. St. Alp's attracts a young crowd.

In the city:

2131 South Archer Avenue, Chicago, Illinois
PHONE: 312.842.1886
HOURS: Daily 11:00 a.m. to midnight

"Is there no Latin word for tea?
Upon my soul, if I had known that
I would have let the vulgar stuff alone."
—HILAIRE BELLOC

TEA LEAF CAFÉ

Like most bubble tea shops, Tea Leaf Café is popular with the younger crowds and serves a wide variety of bubble tea flavors. Board games are available to play in the café, and local art is often displayed on the walls and for sale.

In the city:

2336 South Wentworth Avenue, #105, Chicago, Illinois
PHONE: 312.808.3668
HOURS: Sunday through Thursday noon to midnight; Friday and Saturday 11:00 a.m. to 2:00 a.m.

"The way you wear your hat.
The way you sip your tea."
—IRA GERSHWIN

TEN REN TEA & GINSENG COMPANY

WEB: www.tenren.com

Ten Ren serves bubble tea, as well as hundreds of types of hot tea. For more information on Ten Ren, see page 80. Seating is very limited at Ten Ren.

In the city:

2247 South Wentworth Avenue, Chicago, Illinois
PHONE: 312.842.1171
HOURS: Monday through Sunday 9:30 a.m. to 7:00 p.m.

*"Picture you upon my knee,
just tea for two and two for tea."*
—IRVING BERLIN

SECTION FOUR

Tea websites

www.adagio.com
Adagio is a comprehensive online tea shop, selling black, white, green, herbal, decaffeinated, and other specialty teas. The site also has a page devoted to articles promoting the health advantages of drinking tea. The user-friendly online store has free shipping for purchases over $75.00.

www.argotea.com
If you can't make it to one of Argo's many Chicago area locations, check out their online store for a wide selection of loose leaf tea and tea ware.

www.chadotea.com
Chado Tea Room is located in Southern California, but their extensive online store is available to all. The online store sells tea and tea accessories, but also has a page devoted to literature about tea, including the history of tea, a tea glossary, and articles about wine and tea.

www.coffeeandtea.com
Another Chicago favorite has a comprehensive online store. The Coffee and Tea Exchange promotes fair trade products and sells these on their website. Check weekly for select items on sale on their online store.

www.divinitea.com
Divinitea sells a wide variety of organic loose-leaf tea, including black, white, green, rooibos, herbal, oolong, decaf, and chai. It also sells tea accessories, including yerba mate gourds and silver straws.

www.dreamabouttea.com

Dream About Tea's website includes a listing of classes offered at their shop. Their website also has information about the history of tea and a glossary of the different types of tea.

www.englishteastore.com

At the time of writing, the U.S. dollar was very weak against the British pound. Just taking the Tube a couple of stops in London costs upwards of US $6.00! Fear not, though, because British tea and tea accessories are available at this site—in U.S. dollars and at reasonable prices. Tea biscuits on this site are no more expensive that what you would find in an upscale grocery in the U.S. So, indulge and for orders of more than $75.00, enjoy free shipping!

www.myplacefortea.com

This Chicago tea shop has an extensive online store for those who prefer to shop for loose leaf tea on the Web. It sells a wide variety of green, black, and herbal tea, as well as tea pots, tea strainers, and other tea accessories.

www.numitea.com

I love Numi's flowering teas—rosettes of tea leaves that are sewn together into round "buds" that open when steeped in hot water. Based on the West Coast, Numi and its many varieties of tea are available to tea aficionados 24 hours a day, thanks to the Web. All Numi teas are organic.

www.octaviatea.com

Octavia sells organic, free trade tea in many varieties and flavors. Their website also includes information about the health benefits of tea, how to brew tea, and the differences between the various types of tea.

www.palaisdesthes.com

Palais des Thes is located in France, but has a user-friendly online shop where you can buy loose leaf tea, tea accessories, and books about tea. The website can be viewed in English, French, and German.

www.paper-source.com
Although it's a paper store, Paper Source sells elegantly, individually packaged tea sachets as well as nicely presented canisters of loose leaf tea by Tea Forte. The tea comes in green, black, herbal, and floral blends, to name several. Paper Source also sells minimalist tea sets and tea pots. And while you're at it, be sure to check out all of the great paper products at Paper Source!

www.republicoftea.com
This online tea shop sells loose leaf green, white, black, and herbal teas in attractive tin containers. Tea bag options are available for most teas, also sold in the Republic of Tea trademark containers.

www.serendipitea.com
This is an excellent website that not only sells tea online, but also presents information about the origins of tea, quotations on tea, the work that the company does with non-profit organizations, and tea recipes! Based in upstate New York, this site is user-friendly and promotes fair trade tea.

www.sereneteaz.com
SereneTeaz of the Western suburbs sells tea on its online store, along with tea accessories and edibles. Spend more than $75.00 and receive free shipping.

www.southportgrocery.com
Southport Grocery's online store has a small selection of loose leaf tea. It also sells gift baskets and specialty grocery items such as cheese, spices, baking items, and chocolate, to name just several.

www.specialteas.com
This site sells only loose leaf tea in many varieties, such as decaffeinated, green, black, Chinese, fruit blends, and herbal. Learn brewing tips and how to store tea.

www.stellarianaturalhealth.com

Stellaria Natural Health is based in Chicago and offers naturopathic medicine, acupuncture, counseling, bodywork, yoga, t'ai chi, belly dance, meditation, nutrition, and natural living. It also sells dozens of teas, all of which are sold according to their health benefits. The site lists all the teas they sell and the price per ounce.

www.teacraze.com

This site will list tea events in the Chicago area brought to you by the folks at Tea Essence in Bucktown. Events include tea tastings, tea tours, tea classes such as Tea 101, and other fun tea-based happenings.

www.teaessence.biz

Tea Essence of Bucktown has a great online store, selling loose leaf tea, tea accessories, and membership to an online tea club. The site is user-friendly and also includes a tea newsletter.

www.teagschwendner.com

Navigate to the North American section and find yourself in an extensive online tea store. Whether you're looking for oolong or fruit or black tea, Tea Gschwendner has it all. Look for their clearance and gift set pages to find that special something.

www.teamap.com

Find the latest news about tea shops in your area or around the country. Enter a state and a comprehensive list of tea shops appears, as do listings of recently closed tea shops.

www.teavana.com

More than 100 types of loose leaf tea, including rooibos, black, white, and green tea can be bought from Teavana's online store. Also for sale on the website are Asian style tea sets, tea books, tea accessories, and membership to their Tea of the Month club, which actually offers three types of tea per month.

www.teavision.com
Suzi's Tea and Café in Chicago has a wonderful
website that includes an online store, information
about their café, and catering menus, including their
afternoon tea service for 15 people or more. The user-
friendly and inviting site also has detailed descriptions
of all 135 types of tea sold at Suzi's Tea and Café.

www.tenren.com
If you're looking for information about Chinese tea,
Ten Ren's online store is the place to go. Besides selling
loose leaf tea, Ten Ren's site also has pages dedicated to
tea preparation and tea history.

www.todd-holland.com
If you can't make it out to the Western suburbs, visit
Todd & Holland's comprehensive online tea shop.

www.virtualtea.com
I love this site because it sells the fabulous Castle
Cairn tilting tea pot! At $24.00 a pot, it's quite a steal.
The site also sells tea accessories and a wide selection
of books about tea.

SECTION FIVE

Glossary

ASSAM is the name of a tea and a region of India that is the largest producer of black teas. Assam tea is rich in dark color and smooth in taste. Often used in Irish breakfast blends, it holds up well with added milk, lemon, and sugar.

BLACK TEA is the generic name for darker teas that become that way from a reaction of oxygen with the enzymes on the tea leaves' surface (oxidation). Many black teas come from India, Sri Lanka, and China.

BUBBLE TEA is made from tea, milk, sugar, ice, and giant black tapioca balls. It gets its name from the foamy bubbles that form from shaking the freshly brewed tea with ice.

CHAI is the Indian word for tea, but in the United States it usually refers to a mixture of tea, sugar, milk, and Indian spices. Some varieties of chai are hot from peppers, while others are sweeter if they have more cinnamon and cloves.

CLOTTED CREAM is the thick, unsweetened, buttery substance that is typically served as a condiment to scones. Clotted cream is British in origin.

DARJEELING refers to both a region in India and a popular type of black tea that is grown there. If steeped too long, Darjeeling can become very strong. It mixes well with milk, lemon, and sugar.

ENGLISH BREAKFAST refers to a blend of black teas that goes well with milk, lemon, and sugar. English breakfast uses Keemun tea leaves from China, and is usually lighter than its Irish and Scottish counterparts, which use Assam.

GREEN TEA usually comes from China or Japan and does not go through the long oxidation process that black tea does. Green tea is lighter in caffeine than black or oolong tea.

HERBAL TEA does not actually use tea leaves. Rather, it is a mixture of plants such as chamomile, rooibos, peppermint, and hibiscus, along with other flavorings, which are often fruit or spices. Herbal teas are completely caffeine free.

INFUSER is a basket or ball that holds tea leaves and is placed in hot water. By using an infuser, the tea drinker can easily remove the tea leaves from the water before the tea becomes too strong.

IRISH BREAKFAST TEA is a blend of black tea, including Assam from India. The tea mixes well with milk, lemon, and sugar.

KEEMUN is a part of China (now named Qimen) and a type of tea, often used in English Breakfast teas. Keemun tea mixes well with milk, lemon, and sugar.

LEMON CURD is a condiment served with scones. It is made from lemon juice, eggs, butter, and sugar.

OOLONG TEA is a Chinese black tea that is partially oxidized. It has a slight fruit flavor and is usually not mixed with milk, lemon, or sugar.

PEARL TEA is another name for bubble tea.

PORCELAIN, also called china, is the material often used to make tea pots.

ROOIBOS (pronounced "roy bus") is a type of herbal tea made from the needle-like leaves of a caffeine-free bush native to South Africa. It is a popular alternative to black teas and can be taken both hot and cold. Rooibos tea is often called "red tea."

SCONES are the popular quick bread traditionally served with afternoon tea. Scones are mildly sweet and often contain currants, blueberries, or other dried fruit. They are typically served with clotted cream, marmalade, lemon curd, and strawberry preserves.

SCOTTISH BREAKFAST refers to a blend of black tea, including Assam from India. Like English and Irish Breakfast tea, Scottish Breakfast tea goes well with milk, lemon, and sugar.

STEEP refers to the process by which tea is brewed in hot water until the flavor is fully infused in the water.

STRAINER is an instrument, usually made from metal, which is placed over a tea cup to keep tea leaves from going into a cup when tea is poured from a tea pot.

WHITE TEA is naturally sweet and its leaves appear light and fluffy. Its leaves are not allowed to mature, thus the white, downy fuzz on the tops of the leaves, which goes away after the leaves age. The tea that is brewed from white tea leaves is pale in color and has less caffeine than oolong or black tea. It contains antioxidants that prevent cancer.

YUNNAN is a province in southwest China and a type of black tea. Yunnan tea has a smoky flavor and is usually taken plain—without milk, lemon, or sugar.

Index, by area

LOOP

NEAR NORTH

NORTH

NEAR SOUTH

SOUTH

SUBURBS, NORTHERN

SUBURBS, NORTHWEST

SUBURBS, SOUTH

SUBURBS, WESTERN

Index, *alphabetical*